LIFE TO ME

LIFE TO ME

BY

SAMUEL BROWNE

Life To Me by Yasad Samuel Browne

Published by Minds of Creation, Calabar Nigeria

www.mindsofcreation.com

Plot 1 Ministry of Works Road, Ekorinim 2, Calabar

Copyright 2014 Yasad Samuel Browne

1st Edition: 2014

ISBN 978-978-53275-0-2

NATIONAL Library of Nigeria

Cover Designs and Illustrations by:

Bassey .B. Inyang

Charles.C. Casper

Contents

ACKNOWLEDGEMENTS

The poet wishes to thank God for blessing him with wonderful encouraging parents because they inspire him to aim high, achieve beyond all expectations, think outside the box, and to aim to the sky. They also teach and encourage him to move beyond his today and think about his tomorrow; that success lies with him, but he has to reach out and grab it. He would like to thank his pass English instructors at Surefoot International School Calabar Nigeria: Mr. Mandel for planting the seed into his mind that he could publish his writings and for his encouragement, dedication, and faith that he can achieve greatness. This journey began when he entered his poem "The Magic Pencil" at the last minute into the Rainbow Book Competition in Nigeria February 2014. He did not win, but his poem was one of the Honorable Mentions judged by educators including a Harvard University Professor USA. He was told by many people that he has something special and that he needs to pursue it aggressively. He also thanks, Ms. Enuma and founder of the Spice Kids for their interview and publishing his poem The Magic Pencil in the Nigerian Chronicle.

INTRODUCTION

Book of Poems by Yasad Samuel Browne is a combination of thoughts and feelings experienced on what seem to be a short journey of life. Even though the author is only 15 years, he has experienced life in America, US Virgin Island, Israel, and Africa (Ghana and Nigeria). So young to see so much, therefore he pulls from a rich pool of experiences and expresses it as he sees it from different angles. He saw the comforts of America and the poverty and struggles of the peoples of Africa. He has a strong spiritual base that has taught him the realities of life, the richness of his African heritage, and the struggles of his peoples in the past and the present. His parents also taught him that change is a personal thing that he is part of the circle of life, and he is a vital part of the links in that circle. To him, this means that he is an angel of change with a purpose in life to make a difference and that with focus, passion, dedication, and commitment to success life is filled with endless possibilities.

WHO AM I?

I am a part of a new brand
All of whom are making a stand
Those in the past have done their part
Toiling away giving others a fighting start

People like Erikson, Benjamin Franklin, and
Martin Luther King have all reached the sky
And now it's time for us to pass on by.

They are the stepping stones
Giving us ideas to build and surpass
I am a part of the new generation
This new bunch will surprise the world
Unstoppable, undeniable, powerful;

I am a part of a great force
I will do what I can in this life
Becoming the stepping stone for the next generation
My children and children's children

But as of now
I am the new spark that gives light
The new generation that will fight
For honor, for glory, for something new.

The new generation awaits.

WINDOWS TO THE SOUL

The mind can play tricks on you

Some of them you believe to be true

All of them could be just games

But you realize your mind could be filled with rage

When you begin to think

You end up shouting and screaming with a shrink

Who would watch your every move

In every nook, cranny, and groove

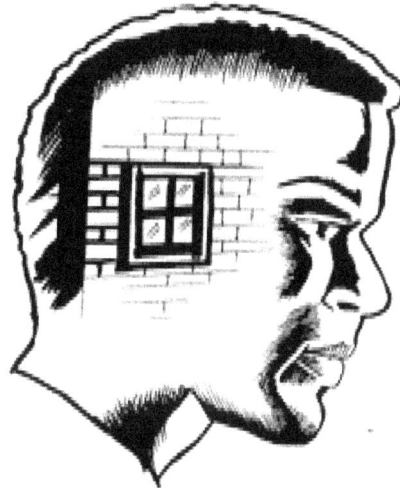

So guard your mind every day

Fill it with science, math, and play

Put some wonders and some clues

Put some love and passion to

Add some knowledge and wisdom there

And keep some understanding near.

Fill your mind with wondrous things

Happy thoughts and kindness

Keep good friends and family around

For you to be aground

And may God always be with you

So your mind can always be there

For you to run jump and play

THE MAGIC PENCIL

What is a Magic Pencil?

Is it not the same as a stencil?

Or is it just another utensil?

No, it is no ordinary tool

Anyone who thinks that is a fool

And I wouldn't consider them cool

I shall ask again, what is a Magic Pencil?

This time I shall answer

And I shall give you in a stanza.

A Magic Pencil is a pencil that takes imagination

And turns it into real life information

And then turns the unimaginable into imaginable

The Magic Pencil is no ordinary tool

It can draw anything and also fill a pool

Anything that you could dream

Take paper and form a team

And let your imagination beam

For a Magic Pencil is used to inscribe

All your wonders which you describe

Write what you wish

For it may be like a dish

Filled with various foods

Just as the heart with different moods

With different flavors and glow

Carrying all of your ideas like a tow

The Magic Pencil comes to save the day

When you have an idea you would not like to go astray

Or if you like your ideas to come out and play

While you sleep, relax, and pray

All of your ideas could be kept secured

So that everyone could endure

All of your brilliance

That could be read as romance.

The Magic Pencil is a pencil that has been hidden for ages

And we have found out that it's not locked in cages

But the only way to find it is with a creative mind.

So when they ask you about the Magic Pencil,

Tell them what I told you

And hopefully they would know it's true.

THE HUMAN MIND

REFLECTIONS OF YOU

You look into a mirror

Looking at your self

Examining your twists and turns

Your body language

Your feet and legs

Then to your stomach

That bottomless pit where food goes

You move up into the head area

You examine your mouth, your ear,
and your nose

You finally make it to your eyes

Gateway to your soul

And realize that you must fully examine your self

Before you can fully understand how to fix what's wrong

LIFE'S BARRIERS

Standing there big and tall

Don't sit on it or you might fall;

It's there to block all your dreams and aspirations

Put there to block you from visiting any other nations

Put there to keep people from getting in and you getting out

Put there until you look very thin and tall

Put there to make sure you do not win anything like a piece of tin

Dull is the wall

Useless and bulky as well as tall

Hopefully one day you can get over it

So finally you will fulfill everything you have lost

And enjoy all the things you love most

But until then, all you see is the wall

Standing there big and tall

THOUGHTS

You know you have them when you shiver

When you have one you just want to let it out

And tell everyone what it is all about

It may be good or it may be bad

It may make people happy or just make them sad

But all that matters is that you have a thought

Or idea that no one else could have bought

So keep thinking and expressing your ideas, state your name

Because your thoughts might bring you both riches and fame

THE DOOR

You must be wondering, what is The Door?

And you must be wondering what it is for

For one, there are many doors

Not just one or two its more.

There is the door between life and death

One gives you hope, the other takes your breath

There are doors for past, present, and future

In one you shall see all your accomplishments and mistakes

In another you shall see a mirror that will show your reflection

And in the last one you shall see what you will accomplish at greater stakes

There is even a door for yes and no

There is a door of opportunity you must know

And a door that no-one should miss or give up

We humans, open and close doors every day

From the spiritual doors that we open in our mind

To the doors we might never physically find.

EMOTIONS

SCARED

I'm scared of the dark

I'm scared of a dog that goes "bark"

I'm scared of spiders

I'm scared of lions, let that be a reminder

I'm scared of creepy crawly things

I'm also scared of glowing red rings

I'm scared of snakes

And deeper than deep lakes

PAIN

I feel it deep inside of me

Suffering, hardship, and misery

Still searching for it, but where could it be?

Deep in my stomach, I look but what would I
gain

Other than more hurt, more dirt, and more pain

But what could it be that is hurting me so bad

What could it be that is making me so sad?

Something that hurts and makes me mad

That thing that makes me feel so blue

That thing that could be inside of you

Oh God if only I knew that thing, that grips, and whips, and hurts, and stings.

But wait!!! There is still some hope

Just keep searching and I shall find

What has been hurting me all this time was just my mind.

TRIUMPHANT SONG

Falling into darkness

Filed with the utmost awkwardness

Falling into hardship and pain

I bet you're wondering, what could you possibly gain

Falling into the pit of hell

Where the biggest evil "the Devil" dwells

Falling into suffering and shame

All those who laugh at you must fell so lame

For they know that when you fall

You get back up and you stand so tall

You wipe away the tears of hardship and pain

And when you stand up they learn what you will gain

More Pride, Passion, and Honor, which shall shower like rain.

TURMOILS WITHIN

All bottled up deep inside

Growing stronger and stronger, throwing away your pride

Waiting for the right moment to burst

Leaving you to feel none the worst

All that anger and rage

You only wish to just turn the page

Leaving behind your anger in a cage

But you know it is not easy to forget

When someone has wronged you and does not regret

All of the pain and suffering brought upon you

If so, the best thing for you to do is to let go

Forgive and forget is what the bible says

Once you do this you shall receive much praise

THE ABYSS

There is a hole somewhere

I cannot find it anywhere

I am trying to guess where it is

Whether it could be mine, yours, hers, or his

Such a deep and marvelous creation

Found on every continent and every nation

No one knows where it came from

But just looking at it makes you numb

Mysterious wonders are held deep inside

But by the laws of physics must you abide

You will not know what you will see if you jump in

You may end up in a mysterious cave,

Or maybe find yourself in your own grave

So if you're wise you will not misbehave

And try to jump into the hole to be brave

So the best thing to do is go home and feel blue

And think of another time you knew

Where you can go outside and play

Where you can get lost in the mysterious hole

Where marvels and wonders you've never known

PATIENCE

Tick tock, tick tock, tick tock

That's the noise you hear when listening to a clock

Every passing moment and second you wait

Every second and moment you sit there your blood boiling, beginning to hate

All those long hours, doing nothing

When you could be deciding your own fate

Thoughts processing, emotions forming

Tension rising, sweat falling,

Body aching, mind swirling

As you're sitting there, just brain storming

Tick tock, tick tock, tick tock goes the clock

KEEPING IT REAL

WHY I TRY

I try because I want to impress

I try because I don't want to digress

I try because I want to astound

I try because I want to be found

I try because I love

I try to please God above

I try for you

THE FAMILY TREE

Your family so deeply rooted in history

You don't know most so it's a mystery

Branches so long, so deep, so strong

Roots so deep, so strong, so long

A web of hope contains Adam, Eve, and Moses too

The Queen of Sheba and Shaka Zulu

The pain and loss from slavery we can't regain

But hope and prosperity we can claim

Just look at your family you may find

That kings and Queens are all around

Some are hidden deep within the ground

And those we know will never be found

So keep looking within and you'll realize

A new King or Queen might just materialize

THE FAMILY

The best thing you could ever get

So many people in this world you haven't met

But these groups of people small or large

All stand by you and will never change

A whole group of people gathering together like a flood

Aunts, uncles, and cousins too

Hello mother and father, it can't be you

Many of them you cannot find

But you know they're hidden deep within our minds

So if you may be so good and answer this question

Who are the people who make up your family?

And people keep back all of your apprehensions

I CAN

I can do what I want to do

I can do for both me and you

I can choose my own path

I can also be great in math

I can see what I want to see

I can be what I want to be

I can reach up high in the sky

I believe I can fly

I can take my ideas and soar

I can take my voice and roar

As long as I believe in myself......

I CAN

I DECLARE

I declare I will succeed

I declare I will not heed

I declare I will find love

I declare I will not curse heaven above

I declare I will be the best

I declare I shall not be a lazy man at rest

I declare what I declare

From my feet to the tip of my hair

What do you declare stranger?

Do you declare to keep out of danger?

What you declare is what you declare

But make sure you declare it straight and clear

YES WE CAN

Yes, we can achieve greatness
Yes, we can despite all hatefulness

Yes, we can condemn and unfold
All the mysteries and secrets we hold

Yes, we can rule and oversee
The entire world, which is full of mystery

Yes, we can shine bright in the dark
Create a new journey which we will embark

Yes, we can be the best
Above all and nothing less

Yes, we can

LIFE

Life is like a roller coaster

You have your ups

You have your downs

Your all abounds

And your loopy loops

You have your problems, conflicts, depressions and hardships

You just want to end it

Get it over with it

And just get off it

But when your time is near

And the ride is about to end

You realize that you want to do it all over again

RACE, RELIGION, & RICHES

What really is so important that you must fight one another to obtain?

What is so important that you must lie, cheat, and steal from those who are close to you,

What will you gain?

God made this world and gave us the opportunity to live, love, and laugh.

Instead we humans have created a world full of hate, anger, and jealousy.

A word where people fight tooth and nail to achieve material wealth to support themselves.

This world is so corrupt; people would even kill their own blood or cast them away so that they themselves can thrive.

Personally, I think that if God was to judge this world, most, if not all of us would go directly to hell.

Man has destroyed the planet God made and is now fighting one another based on race, religion, and riches.

What is so damn important that we must live our lives, learning and loving if we are cheated, lied to, and cast aside so that others can turn this world to dust?

Once man can figure out what is so important, then maybe we can turn this world around and get right back on track where God intended us to be.

IT'S ALL ABOUT YOU

All day I can't help but thinking of you.

You don't have to say a word I just want to be with you,

When I look at you, you make me smile

My friends think I'm crazy, all I say is WOW,

When I look at you I want you to be mine,

I always thought you were beautiful and fine,

My life has changed since I saw you,

This makes me want to be with you,

To sing to dance to sing your praise

Looking at you is more than a dream comes true,

Words can't explain how I feel about you.

WHAT DID I DO?

What did I do to make you sad?

What did I do to make you so mad?

What did I do to make you feel so bad?

What did I do to lose what I had?

Tell me what made you so stressed out

Tell me what your day was all about

Tell me why you're acting so mean

Those eyes I got aren't too keen

I can't read what's on your mind

And even if I could what would I find

Please just makes this easy

All I want to know is

What did I do to make you so sad?

WE ARE FREE

We are a growing world, we all have ideas and we shall promote change.

No matter what color or what race, there will be change, there will be improvement, and there will be progress.

Martin Luther King Jr said "I have a dream". Just those few words sparked a path for a new generation of people Blacks and Whites who brought forth ideas to build upon, new theories, new success stories, and new inventions.

The first Black President of the United States of America Barak Obama said "Yes we can" and so we did.

Now we are in positions of power and can influence the next generation to be more ambitious, more successful, and more powerful.

We've built upon that first dream that one day we will live in a nation where we will not be judged by the color of our skin but by the contents of our character.

We have overcome and made that dream a reality and so we let freedom reign despite of and in spite of modern day oppression, discrimination, segregation, injustices, and inequalities.

We will let freedom reign in America, Africa, Europe, Spain, Russia, China, and all over the world. I declare we will remain free.

I RULE

I said I rule

Anyone who oppose is a fool

Yes I said I rule

All of those who hate aren't cool

I said I control the world

I got all the money and all the girls

I said that I'm the best

Better than 1, 2, 3, and the rest

Yep I said I'm the king

I'm only 15 and I ain't got no ring

Yep, I said that I'm the best

That's right number one in the entire nest

King of kings

I am the leader of all things

MOTHER EARTH

THE WIND

With no leader to claim it

With no master to calm it

With no one to direct it,

The wind is powerful and free

Free to go wherever it wants to be

From Europe to Africa

From America to Asia

The wind is anywhere and everywhere

It doesn't have a voice so you won't hear it speaks and tells you I am here

I am that wind that is everywhere

You can't calm, claim, or tame the powerful free spirit that I am.

PLACE FULL OF DREAMS

The sky is wide

The sky is blue

The sky is full of pride

I'm sure you are too

The sky is the limit they say

The sky is just the beginning I pray

There is no end to the sky

There is a limit to how far you and I can fly

So when you feel sad and blue

Just stand still and

Look up at the sky

Where limitless potentials lie

GOD'S FURY

Wonderful in many ways

Earthly in appearance

Accepted by all

Touched by the will of God

Heavenly in all cases

Essential to human life

Rampant and can cause mayhem

Weather, a world changing event that contains both life and death

Mysterious force that man shall never control

Phenomenon that shall not be tarnished by the hand of man.

FIRE

Burns bright in the moonlight

Wouldn't look as good in the sunlight

Fire brings both beauty and pain

Its heat is both intense and insane

Its heat is beautiful and great

But don't let it spread or it's too late

For once it spreads it burns everything in sight

But its light can shine so beautiful and bright

DEDICATED TO WOMEN

LET HER BE

Let her be who she wants to be

Let her be that child of prophecy

Because SHE IS FREE!!!

Free to be a girl

Free to rule the world

Free to go to school

And free to be a fool

Free to love who she wants to love

Free to hate who she wants to hate

Free to become a Doctor, Lawyer, Scientist, Pastor, Rabbi, Muslim or a Maid

Free to laugh, cry, or rejoice of being made by the hands of the mighty Creator

Who allowed her to be who she wants to be?

From the ribs of man God made woman

To help and stand with you side by side

To ease your burdens and your pain

To help and strengthen you when you fail

In the past many mistakes were made

But those were choices the creator allowed her to make

His punishment was for her to submit but not to be your reason to hate

So......... Let her be bone of your bone and flesh of your flesh

Let her see a wonderful world where you both can relate

Fill it with beauty as you create

A wonderful world where she can be the person God intended her to be

Inspired by the Browne family and written to all women fighting to be free

The African Nightmare

EBOLA

Dangerous and Deadly

Harmful and Unfriendly

This disease can destroy us all

Every country, every nation will fall

If everyone doesn't come together

And help to stop this disease forever

Thousands of lives have already been taken

Family members of the dead lay awake at night shaking

Engulfed by terror and fear

Cries of sadness are all you will hear

From fathers, mothers to sisters and brothers

Ebola has killed hundreds of families and many others

If we don't work together more will die

Only when the world works together

Will this disease pass on by

Ebola will not consume the world

It will die

Thanks

Thanks for all you've done

It has been a lot of fun

To me you're number one

In my heart you're next to none

You are the light in my sky,

The Son

AUTHORS BIOGAPHY

Samuel Browne was born in 1999 in Atlanta Georgia but grew up on the beautiful island of St. Croix United States Virgin Island where the sun kisses the sky and the days and nights are long and beautiful. He grew up an active child involved in soccer, basketball, baseball, tennis, and track and field. However, soccer was his main passion. He is an amazing soccer player and hopes that one day he and his brother are discovered by the national soccer team. He currently attends Florida Gulf Coast University and plays for the Tampa Bay United U18 Soccer team. At present, his primary interests are education, writing poetry and songs, playing his piano, developing video games, and of course playing soccer. His creativity and passion for life allow him to look deep within himself to write. His ambition in life is to be the best he could be and become an inspiration to others.

MORE BOOKS AND NOVELS TO COME